Pierre Penguin

Visits the National Aviary in Pittsburgh

Introducing R.B. Pigeon, as Pierre's New Friend.

Author:
Daryl Eileen Voelzke

Illustrator:
Len Juniewicz

Editor:
Denise E. Sabo

Jr. Assistant:
T. Jared Voelzke

To my readers:

Writing this book has been such a wonderful and educational experience. After visiting the National Aviary, I became aware of so much more about our feathered friends. In my story, I chose to touch on only a small number of the birds that live in our National Aviary. There is so much more to discover that is why I encourage you all to visit the National Aviary in Pittsburgh. You will see nearly 500 beautiful birds and learn more about the various species. I know that you will have an entertaining and educational visit.

To reach the National Aviary in Pittsburgh, please call:
(412) 323-7234 or just come and see the birds at:
National Aviary in Pittsburgh
Allegheny Commons West
Pittsburgh, PA 15212

If your school or group is interested in having Daryl Voelzke for an Author's Day or any type of educational program, you can contact her by writing to:

Daryl Eileen Voelzke
P.O. Box 3074
Cranberry Township, PA 16066

A special thank you is extended to the National Aviary in Pittsburgh for permission for the use of their name and logo in this publication.

Publisher: Daryl Eileen Voelzke
ISBN 0-9630803-1-8
Copyright© 1994 Daryl Eileen Voelzke
All Rights Reserved

Printed in U.S.A.

05/17/15   12/05/93

This book is dedicated to the memory of my father
Robert Butzler, the real R.B.

I'll love you forever, Dad.

*O' THAT I HAD WINGS LIKE A DOVE,
I WOULD FLY AWAY AND BE AT REST.*
                                    -Psalms 55

It was a beautiful snow-filled winter evening when R.B. Pigeon decided to make his rounds of the city. As he flew past a large building, he caught a glimpse of an interesting sight inside one of the windows. "Well I'll be! That little guy is in the wrong place, if you ask me."

R.B. was speaking about Pierre, a little penguin, who due to a mix-up had been staying inside one of Pittsburgh's many buildings. "I think I'll go and see if he needs my help." Sure enough R.B. set out to see if Pierre needed to be rescued.

The tough old pigeon flew closer to the window determined to get Pierre's attention. The little penguin was startled to see someone approaching him.

Even though Pierre was used to keeping out of sight, he loved to look out the window to see the snow falling, because it reminded him of home. On this special night he was to meet R.B.

"Hi! My name is Pierre. Who are you?" he yelled through the window.

"I can't hear you my boy. My hearing is not what it used to be. **OPEN THE WINDOW!**" R.B. shouted.

"Oh alright, I'll try." With all of the strength a little penguin could muster, he pushed and pushed until the window suddenly popped open.

"Good job, lad! Now, what did you say?"

"I said, **HI! I'M PIERRE PENGUIN. WHO ARE YOU?**"

"No need to shout, I can hear you now! I'm an old-timer from this wonderful city called Pittsburgh. My name is Robert B. Pigeon, 'R.B.' for short."

"Glad to meet you, R.B. What are you doing here?"

"When I looked in and saw you, I thought you were in the wrong place. You know, like a fish out of water."

Pierre giggled, "I'm not a fish, I am a penguin."

"I know, Pierre. I just meant that you don't seem to belong here."

"Well, I came here some time ago, but I have not seen much of your city. Would you please show it to me, R.B.?"

"I'd love to show you. Come on out here, kiddo. It's your kind of weather. **Brrr!**" R.B. shivered.

Pierre was so excited about meeting his new friend, that without thinking, he hopped out of the open window only to realize that he could not fly like R.B. Luckily, R.B. was a big, strong pigeon and immediately grabbed Pierre's scarf with his beak and helped him to stand up. "Gee, thanks, R.B."

"No thanks necessary, Pierre, I am happy to help."

Pierre looked up at the beautiful midnight blue sky and was mesmerized by the dancing snowflakes that were falling on him and the city. He spun around and was as happy as he could be looking at all of the shimmering stars and snowflakes. R.B. chuckled, "Well, it looks like you're enjoying Pittsburgh already."

R.B. appreciated the company as much as Pierre needed a friend. The two, content as ever, continued to walk down a snowy trail.

After walking for a few blocks, R.B shouted, "**I'VE GOT IT!**"

"Pierre jumped a little off his feet, "WHAT, WHAT, have you got?"

"I know exactly where your tour of Pittsburgh will begin!" R.B. said enthusiastically.

"Really, where?"

"The Aviary," announced R.B.

"*A what-e-airy?*"

"The Aviary."

"I've never heard of an aviary before, R.B."

"Well, it's like a zoo for birds. An aviary is a place where people care for birds from all over the world. The National Aviary in Pittsburgh is very special, because it is the only aviary in North America that is not located within a zoo."

"It sounds neat, R.B., but I have one question. How could there be birds from all over the world when some birds are big, some are small, some need cold weather, and some need hot weather?"

"Good question, Pierre, that's what makes our aviary so special. The employees and volunteers of the National Aviary work very hard to recreate homes for the different birds. In the wild, these homes are called *natural habitats.*"

"Do they have a place for me? *I'm a bird,* even though I cannot fly."

"The Aviary doesn't have a penguin exhibit yet; however, there are plenty of coolers where food is kept and where you can rest during our visit."

"That will be great, I can hardly wait!" Pierre said gleefully.

R.B. and Pierre had been walking along for some time when R.B. said softly, "*Shh . . .* do you hear that?" R.B. was referring to the sound of the Red Naped Crane's distinct call that could be heard in the distance. "Now, I know we're getting close. We'll be there in a flash, and your personal tour will begin."

Within a few minutes, R.B. and Pierre saw several gleaming glass buildings in the middle of a beautiful park. The park was filled with wonderful old trees.

"WE'RE HERE!" R.B. shouted with delight.

"How will we get in, R.B.?" Pierre wondered aloud.

"You just leave everything to me, Pierre."

9

They soon found themselves standing smack dab in the lobby of the National Aviary eager for their adventure to begin.

"**HELLO, HELLO!**"

Pierre almost jumped out of his skin when he heard a stranger's salutation. *"Whhoo was that?"* Pierre stammered. He quickly ran to hide behind R.B.

R.B. could not contain his laughter. "Don't be afraid, little one. That is my good friend, Archie, the Hyacinth Macaw. Come and say hello."

"Hello, Archie! R.B., he is such a beautiful blue color," Pierre said in awe. "Look, Archie has toys in his cage."

"Oh yes, the people at the Aviary want to keep the birds as happy as possible. The birds get the kind of food they need, the right climate, the proper surroundings, and even toys if they like them."

"C A W, C A W." In his most gentle and peaceful voice, Mickey, the crow, was also saying his hello to Pierre and R.B.

"He sounds so friendly, R.B., may I pet him through his cage?"

"**OH NO, PIERRE!** We must not touch the birds. They are beautiful and interesting, but we must respect them. A bird might try to peck or bite you if it feels threatened. I know you would not want to be bitten by a parrot. It can snap a broomstick in half with it's powerful beak!"

"I'm sorry, R.B., I just wanted to be friendly," Pierre said softly.

"That's OK, Pierre. If you just talk to them in a soft, soothing voice, they'll know you are trying to be their friend. Come along, we have much more to see."

R.B. and Pierre scampered down a hallway and came to the exhibit of the Microneasian Kingfishers. "Look closely, Pierre, and you will see two little birds, who are very lucky to be living in the National Aviary in Pittsburgh. The story of their relatives is quite sad."

"How come, R.B?" asked Pierre.

"Years ago, there were many Microneasian Kingfishers living on Guam which is a beautiful tropical island in the Pacific Ocean. For many years they thrived and filled the island's trees with their singing, but then a decision was made that turned out to be very unlucky for the Kingfisher.

"You see," said R.B., "Guam had a major problem. It had too many mice and rats. Someone decided to bring brown tree snakes to the island to eat the mice and rats, but the snakes ate the Kingfishers, too! After the appearance of brown tree snakes on the island, the Microneasian Kingfishers started vanishing. They are now on the Endangered Species List and may become extinct."

"Wait a minute, R.B., slow down. I don't understand. What do you mean by *endangered* and *extinct?*" Pierre was very confused.

"As it turned out," said R.B., "the Microneasian Kingfisher, not the mice and rats, became the favorite food of the brown tree snake. So many birds were eaten that only a few are left, and that is why the Microneasian Kingfisher is endangered. If we don't help them to survive, they will be gone from the earth forever. That is what extinct means, gone forever." R.B. said shaking his head slowly.

Pierre's beak dropped open, and his large eyes stared at R.B. Pierre tearfully asked, "*Can't someone do something?*"

R.B. quickly said, "The National Aviary is doing something! It works with other zoos and aviaries on a Species Survival Plan."

"What is that?"

R.B. replied, "The Species Survival Plan is a very important project which may stop the extinction of many birds and other animals. Aviaries and zoos from all over the world care for the few remaining birds and hope the birds will lay eggs to hatch healthy chicks. Eventually the newly matured birds will be put back into their natural habitats to flourish."

"Wow!" said Pierre. "You mean the National Aviary in Pittsburgh is helping birds survive?"

"That's right," said R.B. "Maybe someday birds like the Microneasian Kingfisher will once again fill the trees with their songs. As I said before, the Microneasian Kingfisher is in serious trouble. At the last count, there were less than 50 of these birds left in the entire world, and that number can continue to drop." Pierre bowed his head in silence and walked away trying to accept all that he had just learned.

"Don't be so sad, little one. Remember, the good people at the National Aviary are helping. There is hope, and not all of the birds are endangered. Unfortunately, there are still quite a few that are.

"You see, Pierre, there are many reasons why birds and animals are becoming scarce all over the world. There are natural disasters like tornadoes, hurricanes, earthquakes, volcanic eruptions, but people are even worse." said R.B.

"What do you mean?" Pierre asked.

"People are cutting down forests, polluting waterways, and destroying wetlands," said R.B. "They are taking away natural habitats to erect buildings, roads, and other structures.

"Take the Red Naped Cranes, for instance. These majestic birds need the wetlands to survive, but these areas are being destroyed everywhere. Different types of cranes have survived for millions of years. It is hard to believe, but cranes existed before the Ice Age. Throughout the centuries, they kept changing within their own kind to survive with nature's different conditions. Only this time, the conditions currently being created by people are too difficult to withstand."

Pierre said, "I want to help, R.B., but isn't this just happening in faraway places?"

R.B. responded, "Goodness no! It is happening **everywhere**! Every day birds and animals are losing their homes all over the world. If we don't stop this now, I'll show you what can happen. Come with me."

Pierre followed R.B. into an enchanting place in the Aviary called the Fountain Room. "This is a great looking room, R.B. It's a little warm for me, but it sure is pretty."

"Yes, it is pretty, but it also has an important lesson for all of us to learn."

"What is the lesson, R.B.? I want to learn more," Pierre said quickly.

"Do you see all of those bricks that are built up from the ground?"

"Yes," Pierre answered as he peered at the bricks.

"On each brick is the name of a species of bird that has already become extinct and the date when it was last seen. They will never be seen again!"

"You mean, they're gone forever." After a while, Pierre said, "It really makes you think when you see all of these bricks laid out like this."

As R.B. and Pierre were looking at the many bricks, an elegant Blue Victoria Crowned Pigeon gracefully walked past. "*WOW, look at him*! He is really lucky to have such pretty feathers!" Pierre exclaimed.

"Not really, Pierre. Many of the Blue Victoria Crowned Pigeon's ancestors were killed for those beautiful feathers to decorate women's hats."

"I think they look better on the birds," Pierre said.

"Me, too!" R.B. agreed.

15

As Pierre looked around the room, a large tropical bird caught his attention. "Who is that, R.B.?"

"That is the Toco Toucan. These birds have the largest beaks of all birds. Because of their beaks, they don't have to go 'out on a limb,' so to speak. They can perch close to the center of the tree and reach for berries to eat that are on thinner branches. They also can play games with their beaks. In the wild, toucans toss berries to each other for fun."

Pierre laughed and said, "I like to play, too!" R.B. was very amused with his new, little friend.

R.B. thought for a moment and then chose the next stop of Pierre's special tour. "Since we're already warmed up, let's go to the Marsh Room."

"HURRAY, WE'RE IN PARADISE!" exclaimed Pierre when he entered the Marsh Room. Although R.B. chuckled at Pierre, he had to agree the Marsh Room did look like paradise.

"Oh my! Look, R.B., that bird has only *one* leg."

"No no, Pierre, that is a flamingo. Sometimes a flamingo likes to stand with one leg tucked up underneath its body." Pierre and R.B. could also see a Roseate Spoonbill in the trees and a Mandarin duck swimming in the water. Even though the surroundings were very peaceful and relaxing, R.B. knew the climate was much too warm for the little penguin. "Let's move on, Pierre."

As the pair continued their secret tour of the Aviary they passed many more interesting exhibits. All at once, Pierre suddenly yelled out, "**R.B., come quick, this bird is bleeding!**"

R.B. immediately flew over and was quite relieved to see Pierre pointing to the Bleeding Heart Dove. "She's all right, Pierre, that is her natural marking."

"Whewww, I'm glad she's OK," Pierre exhaled slowly.

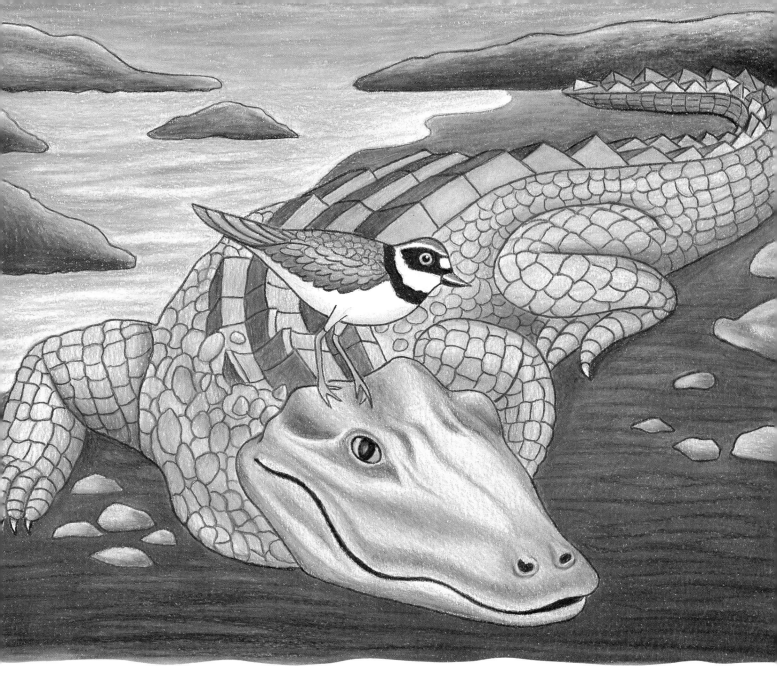

"Come over here, Pierre. Here is a very brave little bird named the Egyptian Plover. If he were in his natural habitat, he would put himself in a very dangerous position."

"What kind of dangerous position, R.B.?" Pierre asked cautiously.

"In the mouth of a crocodile," R.B. answered and shuddered at the thought.

"Why in the world would he want to go in *there*?" Pierre asked.

"He goes in to clean any leftovers from the teeth of the crocodile. You might say that the Egyptian Plover makes a very good toothbrush," R.B. said laughingly.

Pierre giggled, "I would say that is a tough job and not one I would like."

R.B. definitely agreed and said, "Let's go to Parrot Hall. It's a very popular place in the Aviary." Pierre, excited to see more, quickly followed R.B.

"Wow, R.B., there is so much to see at the National Aviary in Pittsburgh. Look at those parrots. They are all different colors," exclaimed Pierre.

"Oh yes, the parrot can be a very colorful bird. They aren't just colorful to look at, they also have a great deal of personality! Some can even talk to you." When Pierre finished meeting each of the fascinating and beautiful parrots, R.B. took him to see another very special bird, the Great Indian Hornbill.

Pierre soon remarked, "I can see why this is a special exhibit. The Great Indian Hornbill is magnificent, but why is he wearing a hat?"

R.B. replied, "That's not a hat. It is his casque."

"It looks heavy," said Pierre.

R.B. answered, "It isn't heavy, but it does pose a problem for the Hornbill. The Hornbills live in the Himalayan Mountains in Asia. The people there believe the casques have special powers to cure the sick. Unfortunately they kill the Hornbill to get the casque."

"Well, at least, *he* is safe since he lives here in the Aviary," Pierre said. As the two watched the male Hornbill, the female cautiously poked her head out of a hole in the enormous tree trunk in which she was sitting.

"Hey look up there, R.B.!
Why is she in there?"
"She is very lucky to be in that big tree trunk. Back in her native land many of these large trees are being cut down, and that destroys the homes of the Hornbills. In the wild after the pair finds a suitable tree, the male covers the hole in the trunk with mud and leaves to protect the female while she is nesting. He wants to make sure that no one can get to her or her eggs."

"Gee, that is really nice of him to protect her like that," said Pierre.

"Yes it is," said R.B., "but I'm afraid they both need more protection." R.B. glanced over at Pierre, who was looking a little pale. "Come on, kiddo, I think you could use some cold night air."

R.B. and Pierre went outside and sat down by the outdoor exhibits of the peacocks, vultures, and snowy owls.

After some time had passed, R.B. heard Pierre sniffling and looked over to see if he was all right. Two large teardrops were rolling down Pierre's little face. "R.B., we need to do something *right now* for our feathered friends. What can we do?"

"Believe it or not, Pierre, you've already begun to help."

"I have, how?" wondered Pierre.

"Just by visiting the National Aviary in Pittsburgh you have seen and learned about these wonderful creatures. Now you, like a lot of other people, are concerned for the safety and care of the birds.

"Mother Nature needs for everyone to do all that he or she can. By simply putting out birdfeeders and birdhouses in *your own backyard*, you can do something that really helps the birds. If everyone, young and old alike, would help, **we can make a difference!**"

"I absolutely agree, R.B. We need to tell everyone to visit the National Aviary in Pittsburgh. The visitors will have a great time meeting the birds and learning more about them. I know they will care as much as we do about saving these precious gifts of life."

"Good idea, Pierre," answered R.B. "It's like a wise old owl once told me, we can all live together happily if we learn to respect and care for each other. Look, Pierre, the sun is rising! It's a brand new day, a new beginning, and now you know that YOU can make a difference in making this a better world."

Acknowledgements:

Frank Moon - National Aviary
Worzalla Publishing
D&R Graphics
Donna Rottman
Linda Sauerwein
and a special *Thank You* to my mother, Olga Butzler, and to my dad, who before he died, was so supportive of me and this project.

Birds of the United States

STATE	CAPITAL	STATE BIRD	STATE	CAPITAL	STATE BIRD
Alabama	Montgomery	Yellowhammer	Montana	Helena	Western Meadowlark
Alaska	Juneau	Willow Ptarmigan	Nebraska	Lincoln	Western Meadowlark
Arizona	Phoenix	Cactus Wren	Nevada	Carson City	Mountain Bluebird
Arkansas	Little Rock	Mockingbird	New Hampshire	Concord	Purple Finch
California	Sacramento	California Valley Quail	New Jersey	Trenton	Eastern Goldfinch
Colorado	Denver	Lark Bunting	New Mexico	Santa Fe	Roadrunner
Connecticut	Hartford	American Robin	New York	Albany	Bluebird
Delaware	Dover	Blue Hen Chicken	North Carolina	Raleigh	Cardinal
Florida	Tallahassee	Mockingbird	North Dakota	Bismark	Western Meadowlark
Georgia	Atlanta	Brown Thrasher	Ohio	Columbus	Cardinal
Hawaii	Honolulu	Hawaiian Goose	Oklahoma	Oklahoma City	Scissor-Tailed Flycatcher
Idaho	Boise	Mountain Bluebird	Oregon	Salem	Western Meadowlark
Illinois	Springfield	Cardinal	Pennsylvania	Harrisburg	Ruffed Grouse
Indiana	Indianapolis	Cardinal	Rhode Island	Providence	Rhode Island Red
Iowa	Des Moines	Eastern Goldfinch	South Carolina	Columbia	Carolina Wren
Kansas	Topeka	Western Meadowlark	South Dakota	Pierre	Ringnecked Pheasant
Kentucky	Frankfort	Cardinal	Tennessee	Nashville	Mockingbird
Louisiana	Baton Rouge	Eastern Brown Pelican	Texas	Austin	Mockingbird
Maine	Augusta	Chickadee	Utah	Salt Lake City	Sea Gull
Maryland	Annapolis	Baltimore Oriole	Vermont	Montpelier	Hermit Thrush
Massachusetts	Boston	Chickadee	Virginia	Richmond	Cardinal
Michigan	Lansing	Robin	Washington	Olympia	Willow Goldfinch
Minnesota	St. Paul	Common Loon	West Virginia	Charleston	Cardinal
Mississippi	Jackson	Mockingbird	Wisconsin	Madison	Robin
Missouri	Jefferson City	Bluebird	Wyoming	Cheyenne	Meadowlark

Author:

Daryl Voelzke lives in Cranberry Township, Pennsylvania with her husband Tom, their three sons T. Jared, Jeffrey and Jordan. Ten-year-old T. Jared or T.J., as he likes to be called, shares his mother's love of writing and worked extensively with her on the book. The editor, Denise Sabo, is the author's sister. The family plans to do more projects together.

Illustrator:

Len Juniewicz, a native of Erie, Pennsylvania, graduated from The Art Institute of Pittsburgh in 1989. He is currently employed as a Graphic Designer.

If you are interested in having Len do some artwork for you, write:

Len Juniewicz
1536 W. 31 Street
Erie, PA 16508